The
Thirty Day
Peace Diet

The Thirty Day Peace Diet

A Way to Unconditional Love

Bob and Judy Cranmer

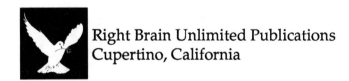
Right Brain Unlimited Publications
Cupertino, California

The Thirty Day Peace Diet, A Way to Unconditional Love.

Published by Right Brain Unlimited Publications, P.O. Box 160484, Cupertino, California 95016-0484.

International Standard Book Number: 0-929009-17-7
Library of Congress Cataloging in Publication Data: 88-60626
Cranmer, Bob and Judy
The Thirty Day Peace Diet, A Way to Unconditional Love.

Printed in the United States of America

Spiritual support by Sister Sundhari Cole
Editor, John O. Willis
Cover and book design by Zena Starfire
Illustrations by Joe Kinnee
Typesetting by Computers To Go

Information on how to order this book appears on last page.

*Dedicated to all the Doves of the World who remind us,
through their beauty and gentleness, of the World of Peace
that is dawning . . .*

Table of Contents

Acknowledgments 13
How the Dove Became the Symbol of Peace 15
Preface 19
Introduction 21

The Thirty Day Peace Diet

DAY 1

Main Course – Opening Meditation 29

Dessert – Write-On 31

DAY 2

Main Course – Surrender to Life Force – Buddha's
Middle Way 35

Dessert – Collect Rainbows 37

DAY 3

Main Course – Mind/Body 41

Dessert – Treasure Map 42

DAY 4

Main Course – Relaxation for Peace 45

Dessert – Word Play 47

DAY 5

Main Course – Love Yourself *51*

Second Helping – You Are a Masterpiece *52*

Dessert – The Wonder of a Touch *53*

Atonement *56*

DAY 6

Main Course – Create Your Private Paradise *57*

Dessert – Pink Light *59*

DAY 7

Main Course – Spring Cleaning for the Senses *61*

Dessert – Rag Doll *63*

DAY 8

Main Course – Nature Walk *65*

Dessert – Gifts from Mother Nature *66*

DAY 9

Main Course – Turn on the Light Within *69*

Dessert – Create Your Spiritual Family Tree *70*

DAY 10

Main Course – One-Hand Clapping *73*

Dessert – Do a Dream Today *74*

DAY 11

Main Course – Let Music Carry You Away *77*

Dessert – Another Way to Tap Dance *79*

DAY 12

    Main Course – Meditation on the Dove *83*

    Dessert – Pleasant Dreams *85*

DAY 13

    Main Course – Nurture Your Child *87*

    Dessert – Affirmations *89*

The Marvelous Tube *92*

DAY 14

    Main Course – Find the Light *93*

    Dessert – The Turtle *95*

DAY 15

    Main Course – Totality *97*

    Dessert – Conscious Breathing *99*

DAY 16

    Main Course – Earth as Mandala *101*

    Dessert – Fan Mail *106*

    More Dessert – Fan Call to a Friend *106*

DAY 17

    Main Course – Hugging Meditation *109*

    Dessert – Time Games *110*

DAY 18

    Main Course – Communicate with a Tree *115*

    Dessert – Make a Positive Difference *117*

DAY 19

Main Course – The Wise One   *121*

Dessert – Stretching Things a Bit   *123*

DAY 20

Main Course – Playhouse of the Mind   *125*

Dessert – Brainstorm   *127*

DAY 21

Main Course – Rainbow Meditation   *131*

Dessert – Show Your Colors   *133*

More Dessert – It's a Colorful World   *134*

DAY 22

Main Course – Earth, Air, Fire and Water   *139*

Dessert – Take a God Break   *141*

DAY 23

Main Course – Place of Power   *143*

Dessert – Let God Do It   *146*

DAY 24

Main Course – Take a Trip   *147*

Dessert – Teddy Bear   *148*

DAY 25

Main Course – Cloud Play   *149*

Dessert – Silence   *151*

DAY 26

    Main Course – Energy as Body Builder *153*

    Dessert – Enjoy Your Energy Every Day *155*

DAY 27

    Main Course – The Flower Garden *157*

    Dessert – Delight in a Plant *159*

DAY 28

    Main Course – Radiating Your Light *161*

    Dessert – Be a Star *162*

DAY 29

    Main Course – Take a Walk for Someone Else *163*

    Dessert – Replenish Yourself *164*

Symptoms of Inner Peace *166*

DAY 30

    Main Course – Peace *169*

    Dessert – Say "Thank you" *170*

Afterthoughts

    Maintenance Diet *177*

    Meditation and Prayer *181*

    Turning on Your Power Through Networking *185*

    Promoting Peace with Resonating Core Groups *189*

    Bibliography *193*

    How to Order This Book

Acknowledgments

We acknowledge all the great spiritual teachers and political leaders who have had the courage to stand up against the currents of complacency and allow their lives to be living examples of the Spirit of Truth. For only when the Spirit of Truth is the inner guide in all our words and actions will the outer world come into peaceful alignment with God's Divine Will. We acknowledge that this Divine Will is what is guiding us and all those who are actively striving to bring peace into their lives and onto the planet. We see that only by merging our little wills with this Divine Will shall peace reign supreme on Earth, as it is in Heaven. So be it.

14

How the Dove Became the Symbol of Peace

When God decided to teach the people by sending the flood, God told Noah to save himself and his family by building an ark.

All the animals gathered around. They had heard about the ark and were told that Noah could take only the best of all creatures. So the animals competed with each other, boasting about themselves and putting the other animals down, hoping this would get Noah's attention.

The lion roared, "I am the king of the jungle. I am the strongest. You surely want to save me!"

The elephant trumpeted, "I am the biggest! Save me!"

The fox barked out, "I am the most clever. Being clever is much more important than being big or strong."

The monkey screamed, "I am the only one that climbs trees."

"Oh, yeah? How about me!" cried the squirrel.

Each animal in turn made its pitch to be included in the ark. There was much competition and anger between all the animals – except the dove. Noah noticed that the dove was sitting on a tree, being very quiet. It wasn't trying to compete.

"Why are you being so quiet?" Noah asked the dove. "Why aren't you boasting about yourself?"

"I don't see myself as being any better than anyone else. Each one of us has something that the others don't have. It is something God has given to us."

Noah exclaimed, "The dove is right. No one needs to boast or compete with another. God has told me to take two of every animal." Hearing this, the animals were all very relieved. The bickering stopped.

Then Noah announced, "God has told me to pick one of you as my messenger. Because the dove has been quiet and peaceful, I pick the dove to be my messenger."

The rains came. It rained and rained. The rain went on for forty days and forty nights, flooding the entire world.

When the rains stopped, Noah called the dove and sent it out to fly throughout the world and bring back word of what she saw. When the dove finally returned, she had an olive branch in her beak. Noah knew then that the waters had gone.

Soon the land was dry and everyone left the ark to rebuild the earth according to God's vision of love, peace and harmony among all His creation. God told all the people and animals to live in harmony with His natural laws of caring for one another, as one big loving family on the planet.

Since that time, the dove has been a symbol of peace for all people of the world. The dove still lives very happily, without fighting. Its soft, gentle, loving expression reminds us of God's ancient promise, and our responsibility to care for one another and this earth, our home. And that is why the dove is called the bird of peace.

Preface

"Peace will not be based on the fear of war, but on the love of peace. It will not be abstaining from an act, but the coming of a state of mind."

Herman Wouk

Peace is a state of mind. This book was written to help all of us achieve that state of mind.

Beginning in the summer of 1986, we became actively and deeply involved in a personal search for peace. We joyfully joined millions of others around the planet in the World Instant of Cooperation on December 31, 1986. We also participated in the next world-wide event, Harmonic Convergence, on August 16 and 17, 1987. And we eagerly awaited World Peace Day on December 31, 1987.

In the meantime, we meditated and visualized peace. We joined the Planetary Commission and Global Family. Through Global Family, we became part of a process called the Resonating Core Group. More about these groups is presented in *Afterthoughts* on page 189. With all these personal and group meditations, we soon realized that peace begins inside each of us and ripples outward into the world in concentric circles of magnetic force.

One day Bob said, "What can people do in between these major events to further peace on a daily basis?" We quickly came up with the idea of a series of meditations and actions dedicated to inner and outer peace. Since our culture is so interested in diets and self-improvement, and since it takes about thirty days to establish a habit, the idea came to us to do a thirty-day peace diet.

Thirty days dedicated to tranquility, both privately and publicly, could be a wise investment for our time.

In thirty days, you can lose pounds of world-weariness, bottled-up emotions, and feelings of helplessness and despair. You can feel empowered in the knowledge that everyday you are making a valuable contribution to world peace.

And in thirty days, you can feel lighter and happier as the radiance of God's love fills your whole being. Peace to you all.

Bob and Judy Cranmer
Cupertino, California
October 1987

Introduction

All of us are attracted to peace, love, joy and harmony. Our deepest nature is peaceful. We strive to love, to give, to serve. And we are disturbed, angry or hurt when this natural desire is blocked. Our pain, hurt, depression, despair, resentment or desire to hurt others is actually a natural effect of a world that is very out-of-balance with the Universe's Law of One.

We are all One. We are one humanity, one family, one people on a planet orbiting in space within a solar family of planets. And our solar family is orbiting in a galactic family which, in turn, is part of a vast Universal family. We are all connected. What we do to one, affects all.

At the moment, life on planet Earth is filled with strife and war. People feel separate from God. These feelings of separation are in conflict with our hearts and our natural selves.

Your natural self is like an innocent, playful child that dwells within you. This child keeps the heart and spirit of a little one throughout your entire grown-up life. Your child plays while you are intently serious. It is a wellspring of hope, vision and wisdom. This child is the source of knowing that peace is possible. It sees all people as equally important, be they black, white, Russian, Chinese or American. Your child trusts that the grown-up world will make peace, because any other possibility is too painful to consider.

Instead, your child whispers longings into your ears, and entreats you to open your heart. It shows you the pain of thinking you are separate from your neighbors, and keeps you focused on peace, love and joy.

This inner child loves everyone and feels a special kinship with other children. (Have you ever wondered why babies are so irresistible?) Every child loves to play and each child does this in its own way. It likes to run through wet leaves, to give little presents, cuddle and give hugs, and play in the woods. It also likes to listen, serve others, be acknowledged, giggle at any opportunity, and watch movies about love and transforming limits. It loves to meditate and it loves being alive.

The child in each of us knows that peace is real. It knows we can spread peace throughout the world NOW, so that other people will catch peace until peace breaks out everywhere.

The child is your peaceful heart.
Would you like to know the child within you?
I invite you on a gentle journey
In communion with the child inside
Who loves you with no conditions,
Who is there to play,
To give hope to,
To cry when you hurt,
And laugh when it all gets too serious,
Who only wants to make sure everyone lives –
People, animals, trees and plants –
In peace.
It has that deep longing.

What would your inner child like to do today?

Now for your diet!

Peace is a daily event. The activities in <u>The Thirty Day Peace Diet</u> can enhance your sense of peace. By following the easy daily menus, peace can be yours in many ways, on many different levels of awareness. Here are five ideas that can make the diet even more effective for you:

1.   Although you can do <u>The Thirty Day Peace Diet</u> alone, consider asking another person, or several other people, to do the diet with you. There is tremendous power in sharing and supporting one another. You may even want to start a core group. See page 189 for further information about core groups. We have also provided information about networking for those who want to become involved in peace activities on a broader scale.

2.   Whether you do the diet alone or with others, you may want to tape the main courses the night before. This procedure gives an easier flow to the meditations, so when you listen with your eyes closed, you are able to digest the activities more easily. Of course, you can mix and match the appetizer, main course and dessert from different days.

3.   As with all diets, some dishes may taste delicious, while others may not be so palatable. Some days bring second helpings or extra treats, while other days are

followed by journal writing processes. Lined journal pages are provided for these processes. Vary the menu as you see fit and, by all means, help yourself to seconds. After all, life is a smorgasbord and this is all Soul Food!

4.   Repeat the day's meditation or visualization at bedtime if it is an appropriate one for that. Otherwise, repeat a previous meditation, that is appropriate, at bedtime.

5.   Don't rush through this book. Take a full 30 days or more to read it and to do the daily meditations.

A personal word about meditation from Judy Cranmer:

"My best time to meditate is early in the
morning, while my ego is still asleep.
I am awake then, but quiet and at rest.
My mind has not begun its daily agenda
and is open to the power and majesty of
the silence. God speaks to me then in
many ways.

"I wear loose-fitting clothing when I
meditate and sit with my spine straight,
arms and legs uncrossed. When I first began
meditating, I played soft music, and some-

times I burned incense. I breathed deeply at first; now I let the breath move as it will.

"Other favored meditation times for me are at noon before lunch and shortly before bedtime.

"Meditation is the most useful habit I've acquired. It is a way to inner peace."

One final note: Keep in mind that our own personal internal preparations are the beginnings of the larger, planetary peace process. In our own lives, let us begin with centering ourselves in an inner meditation of peace that surrounds and infuses all our thoughts, words and actions. Next, let us make contact with others, combining our loving, peaceful energies and moving outward in whatever ways we feel moved to spread this peace.

In this way, the path of peace begins with each one of us, every moment! We acknowledge you as we walk this path together.

The
Thirty Day
Peace Diet

28

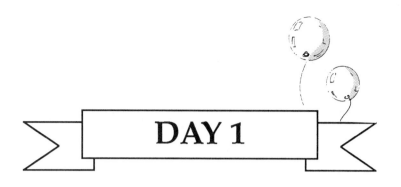

DAY 1

Appetizer

I want to know God's thoughts . . .
the rest are details.

Albert Einstein

Main Course
Opening Meditation

This is the springboard to unlimited possibilities. Be comfortable and relaxed with arms, legs, feet and fingers uncrossed. You can sit in a chair or on the floor, but your spine should be straight. The best times to meditate are just after rising in the morning and just before going to bed at night. An empty stomach will help you be alert. It is also helpful to have quiet surroundings. Stay passive. Let your thoughts flow through the open window of your mind. Let yourself be the quiet observer.

The observer doesn't judge or enter into a mental dialogue or emotional exchange. If this happens, gently bring yourself back into the passive, observant state. Don't be frustrated if your mind wanders quite a bit. This is natural for most people. Be patient with yourself.

Repeat a simple one-syllable word such as "now," "all," "one," "Om," "yes." These mantras are a focal point for making contact with your Source. Repeat the mantra with your breathing. Experiment with repeating the mantra as you breathe in and out. Find a system that works for you and stick to that. Example: breathe in – Om, breathe out – Om.

When your mind drifts, gently let the thoughts float by like clouds and come back to your mantra. When your mind is quiet, stop repeating the mantra and let your mind be. Experience the stillness as long as you can. At the end of the meditation, sit quietly for a minute with your eyes closed. Open your eyes and sit quietly for another minute. Come back slowly from the meditation, moving your toes, fingers, ankles, hands, legs, arms. Twist your torso from side to side gently. Then stretch your body over your legs and, finally, both hands over your head. When you feel completely present in your body, slowly get up from your seated position. Slowly increase your meditation time to as much as 20 minutes, twice a day.

Dessert
Write-On

Immediately following a meditation is a good time to write anything that comes bubbling up from your free, peaceful mind. Write down these ideas, inspirations, goals, dreams, and achievements on the following journal pages. You can also carry a small notebook and jot down ideas as they come to you during the day. It's fun to keep track of these gifts from your Higher Self.

Review these meditation thoughts at bedtime.

Write-on Meditation Thoughts

I want to live a vibrant,
healthy loving life
I desire the light of the
soul to guide me. The
angel heart will assist
my unconditional love
and light to be all
I can, to love, and stand
in my power.

More Write-on Meditation Thoughts

_____

_____

_____

_____

_____

_____

_____

_____

_____

_____

_____

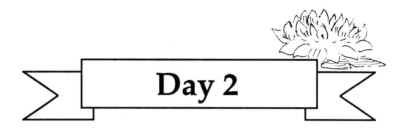

Day 2

Appetizer

Sometimes I think I have fully surrendered and then He asks me for something I don't want to give up.

Anonymous

Main Course
Surrender to Life Force–
Buddha's Middle Way

This meditation can be done any time you want to center yourself, or as a preparation for longer meditations. It can last five to 45 minutes. Sit with your body upright but relaxed, with your head and back straight. Let the undersides of your arms and abdomen feel heavy. Let yourself be gently rooted to the spot with no desire to move. Breathe through your nose, with eyes open or closed. As you breathe, concentrate on the breath moving through your nostrils, in your abdomen, and in your chest. Follow your breath's progression for a moment.

Now, choose one of these three areas on which to focus. For example, I focus on my nostrils. I give all my attention to the air going in and out of my nostrils and any time my attention wanders, I come back to that focus. Let the breath be natural; allow yourself to be breathed. Tune into the Life Force which directs each breath. Surrender all control of your breath. Keep your awareness on the actual sensation of your breath. Feel the coolness of the incoming breath, the warmth of the outgoing flow. Distraction is overcome by practice. Sleepiness is overcome by keeping your body straight and your eyes open.

As you finish, sit for a moment and be like the sky: bright, open and receptive. Notice the energy moving in your body. Is it calm, energized, soothed, emotional? Meditation expands your horizon of awareness. What was unconscious is made conscious. There is no "right" way to feel after meditation. Allow whatever comes into the light of day to be. It is an opportunity to know yourself better. It is a growing, expanding, ever-changing experience, and it is uniquely your own.

Now you can pray, speak affirmations aloud, or conclude with another spiritual process. Stay in a meditative state, fully awake and alert. When you are finished, get up slowly and carefully. Stay with the Life Force all day. If you feel tension building, gently bring yourself back to your breathing.

Dessert
Collect Rainbows

Today collect in your consciousness all the beautiful things you can see: rainbows, beauty in nature and your surroundings, smiles and other loving acts between people. Don't overlook the obvious, everyday things all around you; anything that is beautiful and pleasing to you. Enjoy these things as you collect them. Record them on the following journal pages. At bedtime savor your dessert again.

Snack

"If you could look infinitely far forward in time, if you could look infinitely far out into space, there is no question what you would see.

"You would see the back of your head."

Paul Williams, Das Energii

My Collection of Beautiful Things

_____

_____

_____

_____

_____

_____

_____

_____

_____

_____

More Beautiful Things I've Collected

_____

_____

_____

_____

_____

_____

_____

_____

_____

_____

_____

Day 3

Appetizer
Prayer for Protection

The light of God surrounds me;
The love of God enfolds me;
The power of God protects me;
The presence of God watches over me.
Wherever I am, God is!

James Dillet Freeman

Main Course
Mind/Body

You can do this meditation sitting up or lying down. Maintain a passive state of mind as you say, "My right arm is heavy and warm." Let yourself *feel* the heaviness and warmth. Repeat five more times. Say, "My left arm is heavy and warm." Repeat five times. Say, "My right hand is warm." Repeat five times. Say, "My left hand is warm." Repeat five times. Enjoy the heaviness and the warmth.

Say, "My heartbeat is calm and regular." Imagine the quiet beating of your heart for a few minutes. Say, "My breathing is relaxed and comfortable. My breath is breathing me." Allow your breath to breathe you for a few minutes.

Now say, "My solar plexus is warm and glowing," and repeat it several times. Then, "My forehead is cool," and repeat that several times. Finally say, "My mind is quiet and still." Enjoy the feeling – mind quiet and still, forehead cool, solar plexus warm and glowing, breathing relaxed and comfortable, heartbeat calm and regular, warm hands, heavy and warm arms – for as long as you want. End the session by saying, "I see myself filled and surrounded by the golden light of Universal Love."

Dessert
Treasure Map

A treasure map is a visual, pictured affirmation of what you want. It's a creative way to reinforce a goal and make it more real. A treasure map is a reminder that the Universe wants us to win. It's fun to make one when you let your inner knowing guide you!

Decide what goal you want for yourself or for the world. (A Treasure Map of a peaceful world would be very powerful.) Clip or write words, titles and pictures from magazines or newspapers that represent your desire and reinforce your motivation to make it real. Select a sheet of heavyweight paper or poster board large enough for a background and paste your clippings on it in a pleasing pattern.

Put your treasure map on the refrigerator, bathroom or bedroom mirror or wall where you will see it during your daily routine. Look at it once a day or more and see yourself living according to it.

Don't forget to thank God each day for your present blessings. Place the words "This or something better" and "Thank you, God" at the bottom of your map.

Review your goal and Treasure Map at bedtime.

44

Day 4

Appetizer

If I truly love one person, I love all persons, I love the world, I love life. If I can say to somebody else, "I love you," I must be able to say "I love in you everybody. I love through you the world; I love in you also myself."

Eric Fromm

Main Course
Relaxation for Peace

Lay on your back, arms and legs uncrossed. Inhale and let your breath fill your abdomen. Hold for five seconds and release all at once through your mouth. Relax and breathe easily. Inhale, hold your breath and tighten your entire right arm by making a fist. Tense all your right arm muscles as you lift your arm six inches into the air. Release all your breath as your arm flops down. Do this a second time with your right arm. Now repeat this procedure twice with your left arm. Do your arms feel lighter?

Inhale, hold your breath and tighten your entire right leg by pointing your toes. Tighten from toes to but-

45

tocks as you lift your entire leg into the air. Repeat. Do the same twice with your left leg. Inhale less deeply and tighten your abdomen by making a hard stomach. Let go all at once. Tighten your abdomen again and release.

Now inhale up into your chest; hold your breath and tighten the muscles below your armpits; release your breath all at once. Repeat. Inhale and tighten your shoulders by raising them up as if to cover your ears in a shrugging gesture. Release both shoulders at once as you exhale. Allow your shoulders to widen and lower by reaching gently with your hands for your feet. Repeat the shoulder process.

Inhale and hold your breath as you tighten your face, pulling your eyes, mouth, forehead, cheeks and chin to a point at the tip of your nose. Squeeze your face into this single point, release your breath all at once and allow your face to expand and relax. Repeat the face process.

Gently allow your hands to move and give yourself a face massage – take care of yourself as you give attention to your hairline, forehead, eyebrows, eyes, temples, all of your face and head. Run your fingers through your hair from the roots all the way out as you pull any remaining tension from your entire body out through your scalp and into your hands. Throw tension far away by shaking your hands vigorously. Sink, float, drift and begin to visualize a peaceful, calm world.

Dessert

Word Play

Make a list of words that make you feel good. Record them on the following journal pages. Make a copy which you can carry with you and refer to during the day. Sometimes just remembering a word that makes you feel good is enough to lighten your whole day.

At bedtime review your list of words that make you feel good.

Words That Make Me Feel Good

_____

_____

_____

_____

_____

_____

_____

_____

_____

_____

More Words That Make Me Feel Good

_____

_____

_____

_____

_____

_____

_____

_____

_____

_____

DAY 5

Appetizer

Laughter is internal jogging.
Humor is a free ride to happiness.
Cheer up,
We're all playing the same game.

Anonymous

Main Course
Love Yourself

Take a moment now and think of all your good qualities. Write them down on the journal pages that follow. Next, think of the people in your life and what you have given them by sharing and caring. It might be easier to begin by remembering the people who have given you sharing and caring. It is their love that has empowered you to become the person you are. You are unique. There is no one else exactly like you in all the world.

You are made of stardust. Think of that! You are perfect just as you are, even as the stars from whence you came are perfect. You love and are loved. You are love. Take in a few breaths with these thoughts in mind. As you do, breathe in love and breathe out all that you do not want – tension, anger, insecurity.

Let your mind play. It can lead to valuable insights and an expanded view of the world. If you were a bird, what kind of bird would you be? Is there an animal with which you identify? Do you imagine yourself as a color or as an object? If you were a painting or a statue, what kind would you be? Explore the possibilities! You create with every thought, so let your creation be exciting, fun and humorous. Create a world of love in which to live.

Review your list of good qualities at bedtime after your evening meditation.

Second Helping

You Are a Masterpiece

In your imagination, go to an art gallery. At the end of the corridor there is a special room. It is dark as you first enter the room. Then slowly the lights come on, illuminating a magnificent work of art on a pedestal in the center of the room. It may be a painting or a sculpture, a tapestry or a model of a structure. It could be a piece of jewelry or ornamentation of some kind. It is something the world has never seen before. It is a masterpiece, and it represents you.

What kind of artwork are you? Look at the shape, size, texture. Walk all around the pedestal and examine yourself from many vantage points. Let your eyes and hands explore the masterpiece. Does it have a scent? Does it make a sound? Allow your consciousness to enter the work of art. How does it feel to be this masterpiece?

Spend as much time as you like with this masterpiece. It is your inner self. When you feel finished and full, slowly leave the art gallery. You can come back any time and explore some more, by closing your eyes and seeing this masterpiece with your heart.

Dessert
The Wonder of a Touch

Touch someone with a caring pat on the back, a hand on the shoulder, a hug. Touch yourself with caring. Tell your feet a joke as you stroke them. Make funny faces in the mirror. Massage your head. Hold your hands gently with love. Feel the love of the Universe flowing through you. Share it with yourself and with others.

Love Yourself!
List Your Good Qualities
[Add to this list any time you think of things]

More of Your Good Qualities

_____

_____

_____

_____

_____

_____

_____

_____

_____

_____

_____

Atonement

Because the wide-bodied cranes
Flying south over the bamboo
Are beautiful, I know that I too
Am beautiful, since the cranes and I
Taken together, are only one thing.
Since I remember you with warm rush,
A prickling desire to touch you,
I know that I too am touchable,
Because together, we are one thing only.
The orange and ochre of the volcanic
Sky, streaks my eye with wonder,
And the sky, and I,
Dull brown and burnt Sienna,
Taken together,
Streak His eye with awe.
Blessed be He, Creator of the Universe,
Whose eye is streaked with awe.

Anonymous

56

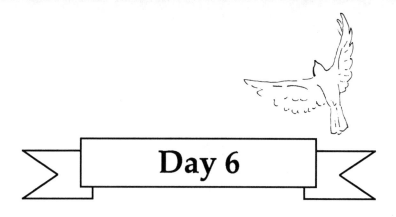

Day 6

Appetizer

The real voyage of discovery consists not in seeking new lands but in seeing with new eyes.

Marcel Proust

Main Course
Create Your Private Paradise

Sit peacefully with your eyes closed. Let your imagination guide you to a place you like being by yourself. This is going to be your private paradise, so build it exactly as you want it. It can be as spacious as you wish and it will be furnished in whatever way is most pleasing to you.

Take time now to create this wonderful place. When you have the basic things in your space, change things around, add or take things away until it feels just right to you. This is your personal domain, a dwelling place where you are protected and loved. You are relaxed, creative, and at peace here.

As you approach your paradise from the outside, a white light from above the entrance comes on automatically and fills you with divine light. You carry this radiance with you into your magical place.

Inside there is a large white screen. Sit comfortably, facing the screen. Turn it on and see yourself there. Look at your physical body, your emotional nature, your mental and spiritual aspects. List on the screen the things you would like to change in your life. Focus on the top two or three. Take the first goal and see it becoming real. See your life with this goal accomplished, and let it become true for you. Take each goal on your list and act it out. They are part of your life. What would your life be like if you were living these goals? Take time to enjoy this vision. Inner victory always precedes outer victory.

Now it's time to turn off the screen and leave your private paradise, but you can come back any time to create, rest or be at peace. As you walk through the entrance, the white light comes on again, filling you with love and strength as you go out into the wonderful world unfolding before you.

Dessert
Pink Light

Put a pink light around the people you meet today. Picture this light as a cloud, a bubble, a balloon, an aura – whatever you like. Pink is the color of universal love. Spread it around.

DAY 7

Appetizer

If you have enough reasons, you can do amazing things. Peace is a good reason. Seek inner peace first.

Anonymous

Main Course

Spring Cleaning for the Senses
(Good any time of year)

Close your eyes and take a few deep, slow breaths until you are in a meditative state. Imagine a broom, feather duster or vacuum cleaner – anything that feels good to you – cleaning out your senses and perceptions. Spend three to five minutes on each sense and perception.

Sweep your sense of sight clean so your eyes are in present time and the shapes and colors are fresh and clear.

See the world with new, innocent eyes. Look around you at the beauty there.

Clean out your sense of smell so your nostrils feel rejuvenated and your breathing is clear. What can you smell?

Mentally sweep your ears, until your hearing is cleaned out, and listen to a new world. Then go on to your sense of touch.

Sweep out your sense of touch. Clean out all the sensitive nerves in your hands, fingers, feet and your entire skin until you feel the air making gentle contact with your skin.

Finally, clean out your sense of taste. Sweep out the inside of your mouth, tongue and teeth, until your palate is clear and sweet.

Evoke in your mind the pleasurable gifts your senses give you. Perhaps you can sense old gifts in a new way as a child might on discovering the world for the first time.

Clean out your perceptions. Let go of negative thoughts and images of yourself, others and past situations. Sweep them all out of your awareness. Feel all your senses, emotions and thoughts become clear.

Fill yourself with love and light from the Universal Source. When your interior housecleaning is done,

62

breathe deeply, open your eyes and sit quietly for a few minutes getting in touch with a new world. "Change yourself and you inhabit a changed world."

Dessert
Rag Doll

Rag dolls function best standing up and wearing loose-fitting clothing and no shoes. Shake your hands, like a rag doll. Let your jaw hang loose and shake your head. Shake your legs, one at a time. Hop and shake your feet. Jump and wiggle your torso. Throw your arms all around. Make noises if you feel like it. Just be that rag doll and let your muscles relax and let go. Do this for three to five minutes and feel refreshed. Do it to music if that appeals to you.

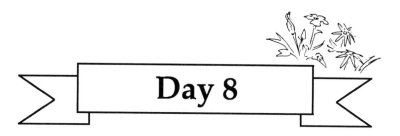

Day 8

Appetizer

What the caterpillar calls the end of the world, the
Master calls a butterfly.

Richard Bach, "Illusions"

Main Course
Nature Walk

Not all meditations need to be done sitting down.
Find a natural setting in which you feel comfortable. In
order to get in touch with Mother Earth, walk with nature.
As you walk, breathe rhythm into your steps. Stay in the
the present moment. It is helpful to repeat affirmations to
the rhythm of your steps as you walk. If your thoughts
drift to the past or the future, gently bring them back to
now. "*Now* I see the green trees and plants around me."
"*Now* I feel the wind, the stirring of the air against my
body as I move into it." "*Now* I feel my breathing." "*Now*
I hear the song of birds." "*Now* I smell the flowers or the
ocean."

Stop to hug a tree and feel its heartbeat. Feel its connection with the earth. Imagine your own heartbeat. Touch the ground with your feet and with your hands. Look up at the sky and notice the colors and the clouds (or the stars). Become a part of all that surrounds you. Pay some attention to rocks, for they have messages too. American Indians believe that rocks are the oldest living things on the earth. Become a wave, a flower, a tree, or whatever else you fancy.

Feel the sun giving you warmth or the rain cooling you off. The earth is living energy. Be with her awhile. Give her some appreciation for supporting you. Say "Thank you" for eyes to see, for legs to carry you where you want to go, and for anything you feel grateful for at the moment.

Dessert

Gifts from Mother Nature

Pick up an object from outdoors and explore it with your senses. Examine it as a child handling it for the first time. How does it feel in your hands? Notice the temperature of your object, the weight, and whether it is smooth or bumpy. Does your object have a smell? Can it make a sound? You might even want to taste your object.

Look at the color of it and the shape. Now feel your connection with this object. There is some reason you were drawn to it. Does it tell you anything about your life? What would your existence be like as this object? How are you and the object alike? How are you different? Now, take a few moments to be with the object, to experience it fully. Explore and enjoy!

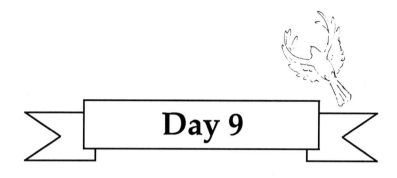

Day 9

Appetizer

Imagination is more important than knowledge.

Albert Einstein

Main Course
Turn on the Light Within

Sit quietly and comfortably. Close your eyes and take some slow, deep breaths as you relax and let go of tension. Now see in front of you a Being of pure light and love. Spend a few minutes sending your light and love to the Being until the space between you is filled with it. The Being is moving slowly toward you now, and the love intensifies as the light grows brighter. You are filled with the light, surrounded by it. There is nowhere that this Love and Light is not. It is all there is. Very gently and with utter peace, the Being moves in to fill the space occupied by your body as the light extends all around you. The light fills your mind and your awareness.

Now you see everything with the eyes of love, and feel everything with the heart of love. Take some time to enjoy the luxury of this pure energy. Relax in it. Enjoy the warmth and peace of it. As you inhale, you take in more light and love. As you exhale, send it out into the world.

When you are finished, open your eyes and look upon a world of love. Keep your light turned on and see the light of others throughout the day.

Dessert
Create Your Spiritual Family Tree

Make a list of the people in your life who have had the most powerful influence on you. Look at the lessons you have learned from each one and say, "Thank you." Send them love from the Higher Self within you.

Review your list at bedtime after your evening meditation.

Create Your Spiritual Family Tree

_____

_____

_____

_____

_____

_____

_____

_____

_____

More of Your Spiritual Family Tree

_____

_____

_____

_____

_____

_____

_____

_____

_____

_____

_____

_____

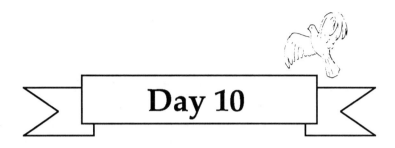

Day 10

Appetizer

One of the greatest needs of the human being
is to be loved. We would not have this need
if love were not the greatest thing in the world.
Without love we cannot live.

Science of Mind Magazine

Main Course
One-Hand Clapping

Sit comfortably, breathe deeply and enter into a meditative state. Touch your thumb to your index finger. As you do so, go back to a time when your body felt healthy fatigue from an exhilarating physical activity. You might imagine you had just played tennis, jogged, etc. Touch your thumb to your middle finger. As you do so, go back to a time you had a loving experience. It may be sexual, it may be a warm embrace or an intimate conversation. Touch your thumb to your ring finger. As you do so, go back to the nicest compliment you have ever received. Really accept it now. By accepting it, you are showing your high regard for the person who said it. You are really paying him or her a compliment. Touch your thumb to your little finger. As you do so, go back to the most beautiful place you have ever been. Dwell there for a while.

The five-finger exercise gives increased vitality, inner peace and self-esteem. It can be done any time.

"God gave us memories that we might have roses in December."

Anonymous

Dessert
Do a Dream Today

List ten things (more or less) that you've dreamed of doing or that would be fun to do. Find one you can do today and do it!

Things I've Dreamed of Doing

_____

_____

_____

_____

_____

_____

_____

_____

_____

_____

_____

More Things I've Dreamed of Doing

_____

_____

_____

_____

_____

_____

_____

_____

_____

_____

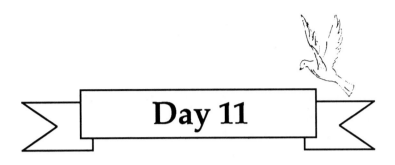

Day 11

Appetizer

If radio's slim fingers can pluck a melody
From night...and toss it over a continent or sea;
If the petaled white notes of a violin
Are blown across the mountains or a city's din;
If songs, like crimson roses,
are called from thin blue air . . .
Why should mortals wonder if God hears prayer?

Author unknown

Main Course
Let Music Carry You Away

Find a piece of music on tape or record that is especially pleasing and relaxing to you. Close your eyes and relax as you play the music. Breathe with the music and follow the sounds with your awareness. Notice where the music takes you. Are you moving fast or slow? Perhaps you find yourself in a particular location. Maybe you are a certain age, or dressed a special way. Are you participant or observer as you follow the music along? There may be colors or patterns to the music. How do you feel, emotionally and physically, as you listen to it?

Experiment with various kinds and moods of music – classical, baroque, new age meditation music, music from other lands or in different languages. For fun and variety, listen to sounds of the ocean, Tibetan bells, chants, thunderstorms; a large selection of sounds are available on tape.

An interesting variation of this musical meditation is to allow yourself to move to the music. Instead of sitting, get up and do a dancing meditation. Let go. Let the music move you.

On the following journal pages there is space to list the music that has helped you on your transformational journey. Some music carries you away and some music helps you to voyage inward. Music can be a powerful tool. Add to this list as you find other music that helps you on your way.

Dessert
Another Way to Tap Dance

Tap the top, sides and back of your head vigorously with your fingertips. Lightly slap your arms and legs with the flat of your hand. Tap your neck and shoulders. Pat your torso, front and back. Play around with intensities of touch. Some places like to be slapped or tapped harder than others. Some places want a very gentle pat. Tap yourself to music or create your own rhythm. Tell your body it's alive.

Music That Has Carried Me Away

_____

_____

_____

_____

_____

_____

_____

_____

_____

_____

More Music That Has Carried Me Away

_____

_____

_____

_____

_____

_____

_____

_____

_____

_____

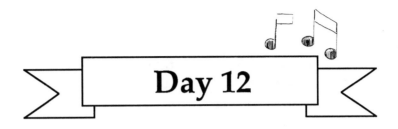

Day 12

Appetizer

Peace I leave with you; my peace I give to you; not as the world gives do I give to you. Let not your hearts be troubled; neither let them be afraid.

Jesus Christ

Main Course
Meditation on the Dove

Music makes it easier to relax and get into a meditative state. For this main course, select some music that is soothing and restful to you. Relax and close your eyes as you breathe deeply several times. Let yourself be filled as if you were filling a balloon, and float like a balloon to your favorite place in nature.

Glide gently on air currents until you find the right spot to settle down. The temperature is pleasant, the air is clean and fresh, and you hear the sounds of nature around you as you relax still further in this place you love. Take a long, slow look at your surroundings in all directions and taste the pure air as you inhale. You feel so good here. You feel safe and protected and in tune with All That Is.

There is a gentle flutter of wings, and as you look up, you see a pure white dove coming toward you. It lands near you and you spend several minutes in silent communication with each other. The dove gives you a feeling of peace. Notice how you experience that peace. Perhaps the dove invites you to fly with it, high over the earth, until you can see no boundaries separating people. Maybe the dove will stay in front of you so you can see its purity and beauty, or it might perch on your shoulder and offer you hope and encouragement.

Let your soul reach out and surround the dove with a golden light as it brings this gift of peace to live in your heart. Enjoy your experience of the dove in whatever way pleases you. Know it will be with you as often as you like; you have only to invite its presence and the dove will bring you peace. Say "Thank you" for nature, for the dove, and for peace as you end your meditation.

Dessert
Pleasant Dreams

Your dreams are wonderful teachers. Program yourself to remember them by telling yourself just before you go to sleep, "I will remember my dreams tonight." Keep a pen and paper or a tape recorder by your bed. If you wake up during the night, write or record the main elements of any dreams you remember.

When you wake up in the morning, before you move, lie quietly for a few minutes and remember your dream. Write down a few key words or phrases; you can go back later and weave them together. Sometimes it's helpful to become the parts of your dream. If you dream of a tree, for instance, how do you feel as a tree? What does this tree represent to you?

Pleasant dreams!

Snack

"There is no way to peace. Peace *is* the way."

A.J. Muste

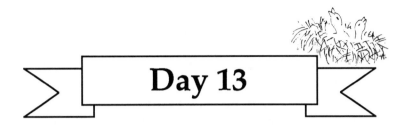

Day 13

Appetizer

Without . . . playing with fantasy no creative work has
ever yet come to birth. The debt we owe to the play of
imagination is incalculable.

Carl Jung

Main Course
Nurture Your Child

Sit in a meditative position with your eyes closed.
Take some slow, deep breaths as you let yourself be
transported to a country road. Walk down the road until
you come to a meadow. At the far end of the meadow
there is a house. Walk across the meadow toward the
house. Notice your surroundings – a stream, rocks, flowers in the meadow. How do you feel as you walk through
this meadow?

Now you are standing in front of the house. What does it look like from the outside? Step closer and discover that the door is open, inviting you in. It is all right to enter this house. As you walk in you realize you are alone. Look around the house. What do you see here? There's a window open at the front of the house. What do you see as you look out the window? Continue to explore the house.

There is a hallway with a closed door at the end. Open the door and look inside. At first it seems the room is empty, but then you notice a small child sleeping on a bed in the corner. The child is you. How do you feel as you approach the child? Does the child wake up or continue to sleep? Is there anything you want to give the child or do for it? Maybe you want to tell it something. Perhaps the child has something to give you or tell you. Experience a flow of communication between you and the child.

When you feel you have finished, it is time to leave the room. Walk slowly out of the house, go through the meadow, back to the country road. Open your eyes as you end your meditation.

You can visit yourself as a child anytime you want to, for nurturing, love, or reassurance. The child can visit you whenever you want it to.

Dessert
Affirmations

Write an affirmation about yourself from three points of view: from yourself, from someone close to you, and from a person who has had authority over you. For example:

"I, _____, am at peace."

(Name)

"You, _____, are at peace."

(Name)

"He/She, _____, is at peace."

(Name)

Use the following journal pages to record more affirmations as you think of them. Review your affirmations at bedtime.

More of My Favorite Affirmations

_____

_____

_____

_____

_____

_____

_____

_____

_____

More of My Favorite Affirmations

_____

_____

_____

_____

_____

_____

_____

_____

_____

The Marvelous Tube

The psychologists we know are becoming more and more interested in the soul . . . what is it like . . . what are its attributes . . . how it differs from the mind, the personality, or the consciousness . . .

We know very little about the soul that can be expressed in modern language, and much of the old is outdated. One thing we do know is that the soul has no container, no reservoir for holding either energy or love. There is simply no place that these two things can be stored. You can expend your energy in the renewal of men and the earth, and more energy will be drawn into you from this expenditure. You can expend your love on the unloved, or even the loved, and the great Source of Love ITSELF will send more love for you to give. But you can't store it. Your soul is a tube through which these great things, energy and love, flow from the Father to the men who need them in the world about you. And you are created.

Father Al Pevehouse

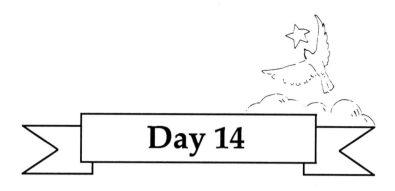

Day 14

Appetizer

We are all points of light, and as we link, light up, we
are turning the world into a star.

Bernard Gunther

Main Course
Find the Light

Very quietly now, with your eyes closed, let go of
all the content that generally occupies your consciousness. Think of your mind as a vast circle, surrounded by
a layer of heavy, dark clouds. You can see only the clouds
because you seem to be standing outside the circle and
quite apart from it.

From where you stand, you see no reason to believe there is a brilliant light hidden by the clouds. The
clouds seem to be the only reality. They seem to be all
there is to see. Therefore, you do not attempt to go through

them and past them, which is the only way you would be really convinced of their lack of substance. We will make this attempt today.

After you have thought about the importance of what you are trying to do for yourself and the world, try to settle down in perfect stillness, remembering only how much you want to reach the light in you today – now! Brush them aside with your hand, feel them resting on your cheeks and forehead and eyelids as you go through them. Go on, clouds cannot stop you.

If you are doing the exercise properly, you will begin to feel a sense of being lifted up and carried ahead. Your little effort and small determination call on the power of the universe to help you, and God Himself will raise you from darkness into light. You are in accord with His Will. You cannot fail because your will is one with His Will.

Repeat this meditation at bedtime.

Dessert
The Turtle

Sit up straight and let your chin fall to your chest as you exhale. Inhale and move your head back slowly. Pull your shoulders up as though trying to touch them to your ears. Release. Repeat four times.

This exercise relieves tension and is particularly good for your neck and back.

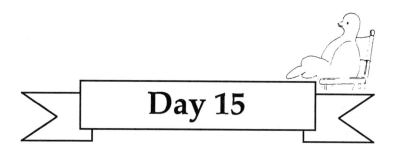

Day 15

Appetizer

People who develop the habit of thinking of themselves as world citizens are fulfilling the first requirement of sanity in our time.

Norman Cousins

Main Course
Totality

Put your body in a chair that is not too comfortable. Open your eyes and uncross your arms and legs. Brush aside your thoughts and emotions and allow your problems to drift away. Be still for a moment. If thoughts come up from the stillness, brush them aside.

Look at the space in the room, and be it. Now be the space outside the right wall of the room. Next, be the space outside the left wall.

Now be all the spaces: the space in the room, and the space outside the right and left walls at the same time. Surround this building with your awareness.

Expand your awareness and be the space in the city where you live. Imagine you are present there. Be present in this room, be present around the outside of this room, be present in and around the city.

Now be present around your body. Do you have your body? Good! Think of a location where you are not at this moment. Good! Think of five more places where you are not at this moment. Thank you.

Now come back to this room. Is this room here? What color is it? Is the floor here? Is anybody here? Is your body here? Good! Continue being still, thinking no thoughts. Just *be*. Be present in the room, in and around the city, and in and around this small, local universe.

From The University of Totology
Hardin and Joanna Walsh

Dessert
Conscious Breathing

This is a yoga technique to wake up your right brain. Close your left nostril with your finger and inhale through your right nostril. Close your right nostril and exhale through your left nostril. Inhale through your left nostril, close your left nostril and exhale through your right nostril. Repeat this sequence 20 times. You'll feel calmer and more alert afterwards.

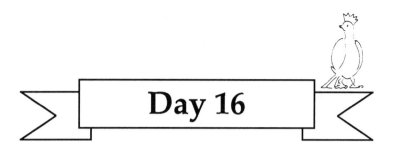

Day 16

Appetizer

Ask and it shall be given you; seek and you
shall find; knock and it shall be opened
unto you.

Jesus Christ

Main Course
Earth as Mandala*

Begin with a chakra** clearing as follows. Sit comfortably with your spine straight and imagine a sparkling
stream of golden liquid flowing into the top of your head
through your crown chakra, where your mind and spirit
meet. Let the liquid fill your head, including your third
eye chakra, the center for intuition, which is just above
and between your eyebrows in the middle of your fore-

---

*, ** Defined on page 104.

head. Wash away all extraneous mental activity. Go with the flow and let your mind be clear.

Now move the golden liquid down your throat, neck and shoulders and relax your tense muscles. The throat chakra is the center of self-expression. Envision the liquid washing away all the things you wish you hadn't said, or didn't say but wish you had. All the tension in your throat washes away with it.

Now let the golden liquid stream into your heart chakra. As you breathe deeply, allow the liquid to wash away all sadness and heaviness of heart. Many of us have developed shields around our hearts to protect us, but these shields also keep us from receiving the healing benefits of incoming love. Imagine your heart filling with a sparkling radiance that opens it so you can give and receive all the love available to you now.

Let the stream of cleansing golden fluid flow into your solar plexus chakra. This chakra is your personal power point and lies between your navel and rib cage. Visualize the fluid washing out your solar plexus and clearing away any images presently keeping you from expressing the radiant person you are.

Now imagine the stream flowing into your spleen chakra which is a couple of inches below your navel. This area is especially related to your purification and cleansing. It is blocked in many of us, so use the stream to clean out the sludge until your energy is flowing freely.

Next, let the golden liquid flow down to the base of your spine, to the root chakra, which is the seat of your body's life force, then whirl around and flow out the ends of your toes. With each deep breath, release all tension and feel your energy flowing freely throughout your body.

Now is the time for real celebration. Transform the liquid into golden light. Visualize the golden light filling your being with radiance. When you inhale, run the light up from the tips of your toes to the top of your head, connecting all the chakras and creating an even flow between all seven of them – root, spleen, solar plexus, heart, throat, third eye and crown. Experience all the chakras as glowing spheres of golden light, fully alive, empowered and balanced.

Visualize Earth as it looks from far out in space and draw this image into your heart. See its beauty as it travels through space and into your heart. Visualize the earth as peaceful and balanced. Surround it with love, and see everyone on the planet living in peace.

When you have completed this visualization, energize it for a minute or two. Open your eyes and rest for a moment. As you go on with your daily activities, carry this peaceful earth with you in your heart.

Mandala: A circular image used to increase awareness during meditation. In Sanskrit, mandala means circle and center. It takes one out of time and concentrates the mind on a point of wholeness. A mandala is a symbol of love.

**Chakra:* An energy center within the body that corresponds with the ductless glands and endocrine system. There are seven chakras, as described in this meditation.

Chakra	Function	Physical Organ
1. Root	survival, personal growth	sex glands
2. Spleen	cleansing, purification	spleen, pancreas, liver
3. Solar Plexus	emotions, power	adrenals
4. Heart	love, compassion	thymus, heart
5. Throat	self-expression, communication	thyroid, larynx
6. Third Eye	extrasensory perception	pituitary
7. Crown	cosmic consciousness	pineal

If you are interested in learning more about mandalas and chakras, there are excellent books available on these subjects.

P.S. There is another, seldom-named chakra called the Clown Chakra. It moves around. Sometimes it is on your ear lobe or the tip of your nose, sometimes on your toes. It could be anywhere, including deep in your heart. It's connected to your comic consciousness!

Dessert
Fan Mail

Write yourself a fan letter and include what you would like most to hear about yourself. Reread it when you need encouragement.

Write Mother Earth a fan letter to express your connection with Her.

More Dessert
Fan Call to a Friend

So often when we write to friends or talk to them on the phone, we share information about the news or invite them to do something with us. Appreciation is another kind of information we can share:

"I know something good about you," or
"I especially like _____ about you," or
"Thank you for _____ ."

Sharing appreciation by writing or calling someone is an act of peace. They will enjoy it and so will you.

Fan Letter to Myself

_____

_____

_____

_____

_____

_____

_____

_____

_____

_____

Fan Letter to Mother Earth

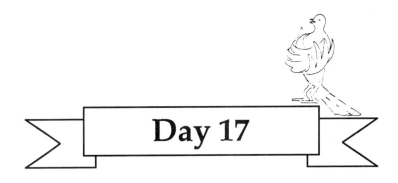

Day 17

Appetizer

There is a place that you are to fill, something
you are to do, which no one else can do.

Plato's Divine Design

Main Course
Hugging Meditation

Sit or stand in a comfortable position and take a
few deep, slow breaths. Fold your arms across your chest
and stroke your upper arms gently with the opposite
hands. Now let your Higher Self say in a slow, comforting way, "You are my child and I love you. You are
growing so fast and learning every day and I am proud of
you. Don't be discouraged, for I am here. I will always be
here to help you. You are not alone. I will never leave you.
Never forget how much I love you and that you are
growing into a higher realization of yourself. Every
moment you get more excellent. I am so proud of you."

Continue to touch yourself and repeat the dialogue. Add to it. Develop a dialogue of your own, adding the things you want to hear about yourself, the things that will nurture you. Do this meditation every time you are feeling fear, hurt, anger or some other negative emotion inside of you – or any time you need reassurance.

Dessert
Time Games

Make a list of the ways you spend time that do not contribute to your inner or outer peace. Your list might include such things as your job, driving, watching TV, talking on the phone, listening to the radio, shopping, attending club meetings, visiting friends, eating at restaurants, and running errands. These are just for starters. Your list may contain many more time busters.

Take a thoughtful look at your list and consider eliminating those activities which seem to make your life less peaceful. Experiment by leaving out one activity, then another, or all of them, if it seems feasible. The aim here is to convert time busters into peaceful prime time. Perhaps you will have more time for meditation, exercise, closeness with your family, walks, bubble baths and hot tubs, reading for pleasure, and other activities that stimulate your heart and provide you with more fun and nourishment.

List of Time Busters
(Do I need all of these?)

_____

_____

_____

_____

_____

_____

_____

_____

_____

_____

Prime Time Activities

(Things I'd like to do if only I had the time)

_____

_____

_____

_____

_____

_____

_____

_____

_____

_____

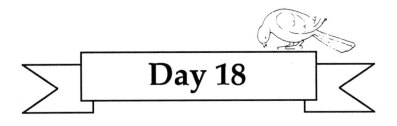

Day 18

Appetizer

When occupied with self, you are separate from God.
The way to God is but one step; the step out of yourself.

Abu Said of Mineh

Main Course
Communicate with a Tree

Today for your meditation find a tree with which
to establish rapport. You will get a sense of which tree it
is by the way it feels to you as you touch it. Perhaps its
deva (spirit) will call to you. The deva is a life force. It is
energy. In Sanskrit, deva means "shining one." Each tree
has its own deva which can teach you how to perceive the
tree's true nature. When you have found your tree, sit
down beside it or lean against it. When you are under a
tree and in its aura, it shares its life with you. Listen to

what it has to say. Trees are sentinels of peace. With their roots firmly grounded in Mother Earth and their arms reaching for the sky, they gracefully accept life. Let your tree share its peace with you.

A tree is a living being, just as you are a living being. Talk to your tree or be silent with it. Imagine how your life would be if you were the tree. Feel the power of your tree. When you are ready to leave, hug your tree. Perhaps your tree will give you a leaf or a bud to take with you. You can visit your tree any time you wish. Take a moment to appreciate and acknowledge the power of all trees. See the many ways they contribute to and make our Earth beautiful. In your heart, thank the trees for being here.

"I said to the almond tree, 'Speak to me of God,' and the almond tree blossomed."

Kazantzakis

Dessert
Make a Positive Difference

Starting today, do something that will make a positive difference in the world. Smile at someone, be the first to speak or shake hands, pick up some litter, call a friend you haven't talked to recently, plant a tree, or tell a co-worker something positive about him or her. The same Love that flows through the trees flows through you. Spread it around.

Ways I Can Make a Positive Difference
in the World

_____

_____

_____

_____

_____

_____

_____

_____

_____

More Ways I Can Make a Positive Difference in the World

_____

_____

_____

_____

_____

_____

_____

_____

_____

Day 19

Appetizer

You never know when someone may catch a dream
from you
You never know when a little word or something you
may do
May open up the window of a mind that seeks the light.
The way you live may not matter at all,
but you never know –
It might!

Author unknown

Main Course
The Wise One

Get into a meditative state and imagine that you are walking up a trail in the mountains in the moonlight. Because the moonlight is so bright, you can see your surroundings clearly. What is the trail like? What else can you see around you? How do you feel as you walk up this trail?

Just ahead there is a small side trail that leads to the cave of a very wise person who can tell you the answer to any question. You take this trail and when you arrive at the cave, you see a small campfire in front of the cave. You can see the wise person sitting silently by the light of the fire. Go up to the fire, put some more wood on it and sit quietly. As the fire burns more brightly, take time to become aware of the wise person's presence.

Ask the wise person a question that is important to you. The Wise One might answer you with words alone or with a gesture or facial expression or show you something. What kind of answer does the Wise One give you? Have a dialogue with the Wise One. When it is time to say goodbye, say anything you want to before you leave.

Just as you are about to leave, the Wise One turns and reaches into an old leather bag and searches in the bag for something special to give you. The Wise One takes this special thing out of the bag and gives it to you to take home. Look at the gift you have been given. How do you feel toward the Wise One now? Say how you feel and slowly say goodbye. Turn away and start walking down the mountain trail, carrying your gift with you.

Keep your eyes closed as you end this meditation. Take some time to examine this gift in more detail. What were you given? Discover more about it. When you have explored it, put your gift away carefully in your memory and say goodbye to it for now. Remember that you can visit the Wise One any time. Open your eyes.

Dessert
Stretching Things a Bit

Take a stretch break several times today. When you feel the need for more energy, stop what you are doing and stretch. Stand up and flex your back, expand your chest, and stretch your arms and legs. Move your head around in a circle, slowly circling to the left a few times and then to the right a few times. Loosen up. Yawn and fill your lungs with air. Let your jaw hang open. Repeat as often as you want.

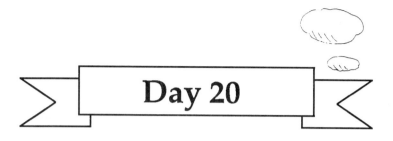

Day 20

Appetizer

You can think anything you want to. Anything.
Therein is your greatest liberty.

Ambrose

Main Course
Playhouse of the Mind

Sit comfortably with your spine straight and your arms and legs uncrossed. Close your eyes and take a few slow, deep breaths. When your mind has become quiet, put yourself in a beautiful, peaceful setting where you would like to be. It may be at the ocean, or in the mountains, or along a quiet river. You are by yourself and it is a pleasant, sunny day.

Ask yourself how you would like your life to be. Imagine your life exactly the way you want it. Your mind is free. Let it explore all the possibilities of this perfect life.

Where do you live? What are you doing? Is anyone with you? Remember, this is your life, and it can be any way you want it to be. You deserve the very best. You can have it all.

Now, feel good about having your life the way you want it. Make statements about this ideal life in the present tense. (Example: "I am living in _____. I am doing _____.") Write these affirmations on the following journal pages.

To complete your meditation, put this ideal life inside a bubble. See the bubble surrounding your ideal life and protecting it for you.

Repeat this meditation at bedtime. Perhaps you will think of additional affirmations about your ideal life. Review all your affirmations just before going to sleep. This is positive reinforcement for the subconscious mind at a time when your conscious, judgmental mind is most receptive. Again, see the bubble surrounding and protecting your ideal life.

Dessert

Brainstorm

Take a moment to think about ways to make your life better. From these thoughts, select one goal that pertains to enriching your life in some way. The following is a creative way to brainstorm your goal.

Write your goal in the middle of a piece of paper. In the space around it, write all the words, thoughts and insights that come into your mind when you read this goal to yourself. Don't judge what you write down. Put down whatever comes into your consciousness.

Look at the pattern you've created. It is a work of art uniquely your own! Now look at the new insights, thoughts and associations you have written down. They are messages from your subconscious that relate to your goal. Perhaps they offer fresh information that may open a new door for you . . .

Affirmations About My Ideal Life

_____

_____

_____

_____

_____

_____

_____

_____

_____

_____

More Affirmations About My Ideal Life

_____

_____

_____

_____

_____

_____

_____

_____

_____

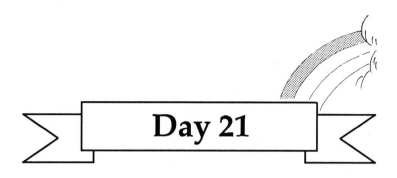

Day 21

Appetizer

Walk on a rainbow trail, walk on a trail of song,
and all about you will be beauty.
There is a way out of every dark mist,
over a rainbow trail.

Navajo song

Main Course
Rainbow Meditation

Sit calmly in a meditative state of mind and body. With your eyes closed, travel to a mystical temple. This is a rainbow temple, sitting in solitary splendor on top of a hill. As you go through the temple doors, you are enveloped in red light. As you breathe in this red light, you become it. Red is warming and physically energizing. It is the color of innovation and creativity.

131

As you move a few steps forward, you are enveloped in orange light. Orange creates a balance between the mental (yellow) and physical (red) planes. It is stimulating to the nerves and lends itself to buoyancy of spirit. Breathe in the orange light and become it. Feel this cheerful, warm color filling you completely and removing any fears or inhibitions you may have. Let them all go.

Take several more steps forward into a soft yellow-lighted mist. Breathe in the yellow light and let it fill you. Yellow is the color of the intellect. It awakens and stimulates mental faculties, and radiates optimism and joyfulness. Become the yellow light.

Next is a green radiance. As you pass through the green light, breathe it in. Green quiets and refreshes the senses. Green is also the color of nature. As you become green you are filled with its harmony, peace and serenity.

Advance a few more steps and surround yourself with blue light. Breathe it in and become blue. Experience spiritual contentment and joy with this peaceful, relaxing color. Blue represents the spiritual force of being uplifted and inspired.

As you move still further into the temple, a deep midnight blue mist envelopes you. This is the color indigo. Breathe it in and become it. Indigo is the color of intuition and spiritual understanding. Indigo represents the philosopher and adjuster of life's situations.

Finally, take a few more steps into a violet ray. Breathe it deeply into your being. Violet is a link from the known to the unknown. Violet is the color of spirituality.

Now look back through the rainbow colors: violet, indigo, blue, green, yellow, orange and red. Is there one you would like to spend more time in, or one that has a special significance for you? If so, go back now and spend as much time there as you like.

As you leave the rainbow temple, you are enveloped by a white and golden light that protects and energizes you at all times. Feel the love and power in this light.

Dessert
Show Your Colors

Pick your clothes for the particular activity you are going to do. In selecting your clothing, choose colors that match or balance your mood of the moment. Colors affect us in different ways.

Red raises self-esteem and gives us energy. It is a color of action and creativity.

Orange and yellow are invigorating colors. Orange stimulates nerves and is very cheerful. Yellow is intellectual and radiates optimism and joyfulness.

Green and blue are calming. Green represents harmony, peace and serenity. Blue is relaxing and emanates the spiritual force of being uplifted and inspired.

Indigo and violet are inspiring colors. Indigo awakens intuition and spiritual understanding. Violet envisions the unknown and uplifts us inwardly.

How do you feel when you wear different colors? How do you feel wearing all white or all black?

Give yourself a lift with colors every day. And, who knows, you may give a lift to someone else who sees you.

More Dessert
It's a Colorful World

Color is an important part of our world. Here is an enjoyable color game to play.

Select one color to notice for a day. Notice how often it comes into your field of vision, both indoors and out. How is it used? Do you see it where you live, where you work, on someone's clothing, in your favorite restaurant? Is it in Mother Nature's scheme of things? Notice its effect on you.

Look for contrasts that make your chosen color stand out. Notice any subtle variations from light to dark in this color.

You may find yourself becoming more aware of all colors and beginning to look at the world as an artist would.

You are an artist, so enjoy the colorful world you have created.

P.S. Do you dream in color?

List of Colors I Like and Use

(Write down how you respond to these colors)

_____

_____

_____

_____

_____

_____

_____

_____

_____

_____

More Colors I Like and Use

_____

_____

_____

_____

_____

_____

_____

_____

_____

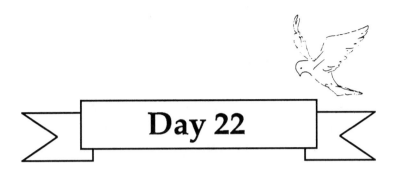

Day 22

Appetizer

What you are speaks so loudly people can't
hear what you say.

Emerson

Main Course
Earth, Air, Fire and Water

Relax and slowly count backwards from ten to
zero. With each number relax and let go a little more.
When you reach zero, breathe deeply and relax completely. Now imagine yourself transported to a prairie at
a time before man was created. Stand there for a few
minutes barefoot. All around you is the waving grass and
a comforting solitude. Feel the earth beneath your bare
feet. Dig your toes into the rich, fertile soil. Look around
you. As far as the eye can see there is earth stretching to

meet the mountains and horizon beyond. This is Mother Earth, from which all new life is created.

Lie down and embrace the earth, your mother. Feel her heartbeat. This is the life force from which you came. Feel the energy and power of Mother Earth as you lie close to her. Now face the sun and feel the warm energy of the source of life as it warms the grasses and shines upon your face and body. Breathe in its radiance and let it fill you with its power. The earth is our Mother and the sun is our Father.

Now clouds begin drifting across the sky, blocking out the sun. Rain begins to gently fall, bathing your hair and body with its cool, cleansing moisture. Exult in the rain that adds life to the grasses and earth. Feel your connection to this nourishing water.

Earth, Air, Fire and Water... All these elements of life are in you and lead you to their source, the source of all life. This Divine Power reaches out now to touch you with life-giving, healing, loving hands. Feel yourself touched by this power. When you are ready, come back to your body, where you were meditating, by counting from one to three. The spirits of Earth, Air, Fire and Water come with you.

Dessert
Take a God Break

When you feel rushed, frazzled, hassled or anxious, your mind and body need refreshment. Become very still. Breathe in God, breathe out irritation. Breathe in God, breathe out limitation. Breathe in God, light, love and peace. Breathe out darkness, pain and anger. Repeat whenever necessary. Then go your way renewed and refreshed, ready to begin again.

(Note: Some may want to use "Higher Power," "the Source," "Infinite Intelligence," "the Tao" or some other term in place of "God.")

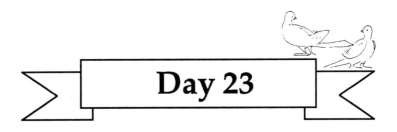

Day 23

Appetizer

If we do not change our direction, we are likely
to end up where we are headed.

Ancient Chinese proverb

Main Course
Place of Power

Lie on your back with your arms and legs uncrossed. Loosen any tight clothing. To appreciate how
good relaxation feels, let yourself feel tension. Beginning
with your toes and working your way up to your head,
lightly tense the muscles in your body until your whole
body is tense. Feel the tension all over. Now take a deep
breath, exhale and relax. Relax completely and allow
yourself to float peacefully.

Now you are ready to enter your Place of Power,
a place where you are completely safe. Picture yourself in

this Place of Power. You are in control now and in touch with your Self. Your Place of Power may be indoors or outdoors and may have in it anything or anyone you want. It is uniquely yours to return to any time you visualize it.

In your mind, turn and face in any direction you wish. Mentally draw a symbol that will be a secret key to your Place of Power. See the symbol glow with a deep blue flame. Take in a deep breath, exhale and enter your Place of Power.

Once you are in your Place of Power, turn and face East. Notice what you see, hear, feel and sense. East symbolizes air. It is the direction of the air currents that circle the earth. It is wind and clouds. It is Wisdom, the power of the mind to know. East is spring, the dawn and the high-flying eagle. It is the butterfly.

Turn and face South. Notice what you see, hear, feel and sense. South is the Path of Life, the quality of will to channel energy and direct power. It is fire – candle flame, lightning, starlight and sunlight. South is noon and summer. It is the lion, the coyote and the thunderbird.

Turn and face West. Notice what you see, hear, feel and sense. West is water – oceans, rivers, tides, and the well of the inner mind. It is the Long Journey, the courage to face our deepest feelings. It is twilight and autumn. West is the frog, the grizzly bear and the sea animals.

Turn and face North. Notice what you see, hear, feel and sense. North is Earth and Cleansing Winds. It is mystery – the power to keep silent and listen. North is midnight, winter and renewal. It is the snow goose, the otter, the cougar and the white buffalo.

Take some time to explore your Place of Power. When you are ready to leave, turn to face East and say goodbye. Turn to face South and say goodbye. Turn to face West and say goodbye. Turn to face North and say goodbye. Now look for your symbol. See it glow as the entrance to your Place of Power opens. Take a deep breath, and as you exhale, leave your Place of Power. Open your eyes and quietly, slowly come back to the present.

Dessert

Let God Do It

This is an exercise in getting yourself out of the way.

If you have some particular difficulty, or a problem to solve, don't think about it. Instead, think about God. Say, "I am going to give this situation (or person) to God." Do not try to visualize God, because this is impossible. Instead, think about other words for God, such as the Tao, Creator, Radiant One, Infinite Intelligence or Allah. Next, think about the qualities of God. God is Love, Truth, Light and Wisdom. Then, when the difficulty has been resolved, drop all thought of the matter.

Idea from Emmet Fox, The Golden Key

Day 24

Appetizer

The future is not a place we are going.
The future is a place we are creating.

St. Joan of Arc

Main Course
Take a Trip

Create a meditative state by whatever means you prefer. It can be one you already practice or one described in these pages. When you are relaxed, close your eyes and begin this visualization by taking a trip to another place in the world. Imagine you are from another country. How is your life similar to the life you live here? How is it different? What is your environment like? What kind of food do you eat? Think of all the possible aspects about yourself and the country in which you live. What is your view of world peace? What is your spiritual life like?

When your exploration feels complete, come gently back from the other country and open your eyes. Reflect quietly on what you have seen, heard and experienced.

Take time to talk to people from other places. Ask them about their lives. Find a foreign pen pal.

Dessert
Teddy Bear

Get yourself a Teddy Bear or some other soft, stuffed animal or object that provides instant calming and nurturing. When you need reassurance, talk to your Teddy Bear. Hold him and let him reassure you. Teddy Bears are very understanding and they love you just as you are. They don't judge you. Give your bear a hug as often as you want. He can become *real*. (What *real* means: when a child loves a Teddy Bear for a long, long time, not just to play with, but *really* loves it, then it becomes *real*.)

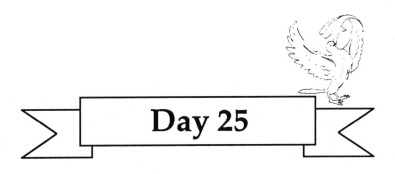

Day 25

Appetizer

Go confidently in the direction of your dreams.
Live the life you've imagined!

Thoreau

Main Course
Cloud Play

Close your eyes. Take a few slow, deep breaths. Focus on your heart and chest area. Envelope it in pink light. Take in a breath. Hold it as you raise the pink light to a place a few inches above your head. Release your breath slowly, expanding the light so it includes your head and upper body. When you've expelled your breath, hold your breath gently as you continue visualizing pink light in your head and upper body.

Next, envelope your throat and shoulders in bright blue light. Inhale and hold your breath as you raise the blue light to a place a few inches above your head. Release your breath slowly, expanding the light so it includes your head and the upper part of your body. When you've expelled your breath, hold your breath gently while visualizing the vibrant blue light around your head and upper body.

Focus on your pituitary gland (third eye) above the bridge of your nose between your eyebrows and one-half inch behind your forehead. Inhale and fill your head with a brilliant white light. Hold your breath and raise the white light to a point a few inches above your head. As you release your breath, feel your third eye merge with the light. Imagine this light you have created lighting up the room. Although your lungs are empty, hold your breath a little longer and let the brilliant light settle around your head and body above your waist.

Now relax and sit in quiet meditation. Before you rise, bless the world.

Dessert
Silence

Enjoy the challenge of spending 24 hours without talking to anyone. You can write messages, but don't speak. There are many ways to communicate besides using words or sounds. Perhaps this game of "Silence" will give you more time to hear your own thoughts.

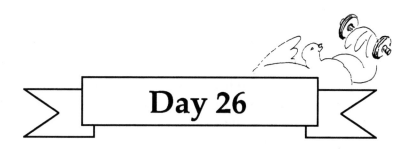

Day 26

Appetizer

When you fix your heart on one point, then nothing is
impossible for you.

Buddha

Main Course
Energy as Body Builder

Energy is neutral. It's what you do with it that
makes it healing or harmful, creative or destructive.
Think of all the energy within and around you! This
energy has great power which you can use to improve
your body.

Begin this meditation by selecting a part of your
body you want to strengthen and beautify. It could be
your abdomen, neck, thighs, buttocks, chest – any part of
your body where you have some control over your
muscles.

153

Take a moment to sit quietly and scan your body. Let the part that wants energizing give you a message. When you have selected an area to work with, practice tightening and relaxing the muscles in that area to experience the surge of energy to that body part.

It might help to recall a time when your body tensed up as a result of a negative emotion. Maybe your neck stiffened, you clenched your jaw, your stomach tightened, you made fists with your hands, or your head and chest started pounding.

Now when you feel your body beginning to react to a negative emotion, such as your own or another's annoyance or irritation, convert the negativity to a positive improvement of your body. Consciously tense and release the selected muscles instead of letting your body be tensed up uncontrollably by the negative emotion. You can establish your own rhythm to this tensing and releasing.

Dessert
Enjoy Your Energy Every Day

Practice today's meditation in daily life. You can do it in meetings, in line at the grocery store, in traffic, waiting for elevators, at home with your family – any time you start to feel harried or tense for any reason. Eventually, you will be able to convert the negative thrust to a positive one, and you will also be able to send it back to the Universe as love, peace and compassion. This is not just an activity; it can become a whole way of life!

156

Day 27

Appetizer

He drew a circle that shut me out –
Heretic, rebel, a thing to flout.
But Love and I had the wit to win;
We drew a circle that took him in.

Edwin Markham

Main Course
The Flower Garden

Center yourself by sitting with your spine straight,
feet flat on the floor, and hands resting gently on your lap.
Close your eyes. Imagine a cord of psychic energy running from the base of your spine into the earth. Close your
eyes and imagine a picture screen in the middle of your
head. Make a picture of a flower in the middle of the
screen, and look at all its details – stem, petals, color,
leaves, and the earth around it. Dissolve the flower and

make another flower, more beautiful than the first. Dissolve this one and make another one. Do this several times until you feel comfortable creating flowers.

Now think of a friend and make a new flower that embodies your friend's qualities. Allow your friend's energy to fill the flower and transform it. Notice any changes in the flower. Create a sun and put it in the picture. This represents your friend's energy. Where is the sun in relation to the flower?

Repeat this exercise for three more friends or relatives. (Another idea is to make a goodwill flower for someone in another country.) Observe the differences in the flowers and their relationships to the sun. Each flower will have a special meaning for you. When you have finished looking at them, completely dissolve all of your flowers.

Now make a flower for yourself. If there is anything you don't like about this flower, just change it until it is exactly the way you want it. Enjoy the flower that is you. Then dissolve this flower. Bring a large golden sun into your body through the crown of your head and open your eyes. Shine on the people you meet.

Dessert
Delight in a Plant

If you have plants in your home, give them some special attention. They might be ready for some plant food. Perhaps they would like to be turned or put in a different location. Maybe they'd enjoy music or an encouraging word from you.

If you don't have any plants, it might be fun to get one or to plant some seeds and watch them grow.

160

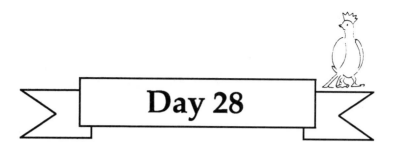

Day 28

Appetizer

A guru is more than a teacher. He is a connection
to God. Be your own guru. "Great leaders are
rare, so I'm following myself."

Ashley Brilliant

Main Course
Radiating Your Light

Close your eyes, relax and breathe until you are in
a meditative state. You, and everybody else, have a sunbeam right in the center of your being. Focus on your
center, in the middle of your chest or solar plexus, which-
ever feels like your center at the moment. Feel your beautiful, powerful, golden sunbeam deep within this place.
Now see yourself as a center of light. Radiate your light.
As you interact with people, see their light and feel your
own light. Notice the lights communicating with each

other. No matter what is going on externally, the lights continue to communicate with each other from their centers.

Visualize various situations you may find yourself in during the day and picture your light silently communicating with other lights. Feel the sense of power that tending and nurturing your light gives you. Breathe deeply and get an image of your light in all its glory and in all its details. When you are in conversation with someone, your lights silently communicate. Don't tell anyone you are doing this. Simply *do* it.

Dessert
Be a Star

We each have our own personal star. When you are walking, imagine you are swinging from your star. Your star lifts your body as you move. Your head feels the attraction of your star. It is taking all the weight off your feet and you just glide along, light and free, carried by your star. Feel your star shining in your heart throughout the day. Look for other people's stars. Twinkle together.

Day 29

Appetizer

When life itself seems lunatic,
who knows where madness lies?
To surrender dreams – this may be madness . . .
Too much sanity may be madness.
And maddest of all, to see life as it is and not as it
(could) be.

Don Quixote

Main Course
Take a Walk for Someone Else

On Day 8, page 65, there is a Nature Walk for you to enjoy. Taking a walk is a wonderful way to become centered. You can feel your connection to the planet.

This main course is an opportunity to take a nature walk for someone else. You may have a friend who is too sick, depressed or confused to get out and walk.

Perhaps you know someone in prison or someone who is recovering from surgery. If you know the person well, notice things he or she would be especially interested in and tell your friend, either in a letter, by phone or in person.

If you report back to your friend in person, take a leaf, rock or some other interesting thing you found on your walk.

You will probably notice things on your walk that you may not have paid particular attention to before. Notice things with all your senses, as you did on the previous Nature Walk. It's fun to be an earth reporter, and you will brighten another person's life, too.

Dessert
Replenish Yourself

This is a massage that will bring new energy to your body. You can stand, sit or lie down, with your clothes on or off. This massage can be done anytime you wish.

Imagine your hands are a magic healing tool. Slowly massage all parts of your head and body that you can easily reach. As you massage, breathe in healing energy into your chest. As you exhale, send this healing energy down your arms to your hands and into the part of your body you are massaging. Go slowly, and continue this massage as long as you like. This is a great way to relax, center and revitalize yourself even while sitting in a chair at work.

Symptoms of Inner Peace

Watch for signs of peace. The hearts of a great many have already been exposed to it and it seems likely that we could find our society experiencing it in epidemic proportions, which then, of course, could pose a serious threat to what has up to now seemed a fairly stable condition of conflict in the world. Some signs and symptoms of inner peace:

1. Tendency to think and act spontaneously rather than from fears based on past experiences.

2. An unmistakeable ability to enjoy each moment.

3. Loss of interest in judging other people.

4. Loss of interest in judging self.

5. Loss of interest in interpreting actions of others.

6. Loss of interest in conflict.

7. Loss of ability to worry.   (This is a very serious symptom.)

8. Frequent, overwhelming episodes of appreciation.

9. Contented feelings of connectedness with others and nature.

10. Frequent attacks of smiling through the eyes from the heart.

11. Increasing tendency to let things happen rather than make them happen.

12. Increased susceptibility to love extended by others as well as the uncontrollable urge to extend it.

WARNING: If you have all or even most of the above symptoms, please be advised that your condition of PEACE may be so far advanced as to not be curable. If you are exposed to anyone exhibiting several of these symptoms, remain exposed only at your own risk. This condition of PEACE is probably in its infectious stage.

Author: Saskia Davis, Northwest Center for Attitudinal Healing, Seattle, WA.
Copyright to: Saskia Davis, February 1984

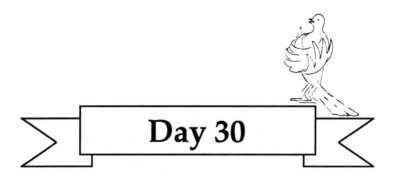

Day 30

Appetizer

We have it within our power
to begin the world again.

Thomas Paine

Main Course
Peace

Sit up or lie down. Be comfortable and breathe until you enter a place of deep relaxation. Let calm, loving energy fill your being. Imagine a world of peace – no weapons, no wars – with all people living in harmony. What does your daily life look like in this peaceful world? What are you doing? What are others doing? All the money and energy that was once spent on war is now being spent constructively to help people live happy, fulfilling lives. See the celebrations taking place, the smiling faces, the end of hunger and poverty. What does your world of peace look like?

Now move into outer space and see our beautiful Earth. See how it looks with no visible boundaries, as a magnificent blue planet whirling through the Universe. Put a golden light around it. Open your sense of communication with other creative forces in the galaxy. Feel the connection with Supreme Intelligence, with God, with All That Is!

Let peace fill your being from the inside out. Extend peace to your family, friends, and everyone you meet. Know that Love and Peace are all there is. *Now there is peace on Earth and it has begun with you.*

Dessert

Say "Thank you"

Say "Thank you." We do have it within our power to begin the world again. Let's start now!

What My World of Peace Looks Like

_____

_____

_____

_____

_____

_____

_____

_____

_____

More Visions of My Peaceful World

_____

_____

_____

_____

_____

_____

_____

_____

_____

_____

What I am Thankful for

_____

_____

_____

_____

_____

_____

_____

_____

_____

_____

More of What I am Thankful for

_____

_____

_____

_____

_____

_____

_____

_____

_____

_____

Afterthoughts

Maintenance Diet

As with all diets, this one needs maintenance to keep you in good spiritual shape. Exercising your sense of inner peace will keep it limber and flexible as peace becomes a way of life for you.

Begin each day with a positive thought. It can be one of the appetizers from this book or an affirmation of your own creation. You might want to start a collection of peaceful appetizers, inspiring words that you have read or heard, or truths from your own spiritual consciousness.

Choose the main courses and desserts that deepen your feeling of peace and do them often. Twenty minutes twice a day devoted entirely to inner peace will create harmony in your life. Form a loving group with several other people and meditate together weekly. Use this book as a guide or create your own processes together. There is much peaceful power in groups.

End each day with a bedtime snack of peaceful affirmations and prayers. A simple "Thank you" is a wonderful thought to send you drifting off to sleep.

Peace is a reality now. It is within you. The purpose of the Maintenance Diet is summarized in these words by Bartholomew:

"How can I feel at peace?

"The only way I know for the human to feel 'at peace' is to have a deep inner sense that "God's in It's heaven and all's right with *my* world." It is a feeling that everything is in harmony each moment no matter how bad the situation looks. With this feeling comes the courage to do strange and wonderful things. When the discouragement committee rises up and says, "You can't do that," you find that you can. The warrior is born within you, and you find yourself daring new ideas to fill you, new roads to call you, new responses to delight you. *You feel new*.

"There is a very deep desire in the human to have other people like you. No blame. Life goes easier if people like you. But an interesting thing will happen, my friends, if you dare to be the warrior and trust what comes to you. Either your friends will respond to your deepening awareness, or think you're totally crazy and have nothing more to do with you. And they leave your life. In either case, harmony and peace are yours.

"But how to get this deep feeling of 'rightness?' Of peace? You begin as you do with any deep desire – by stating your intention. Tell yourself a hundred times a day, "I want *peace*. I want to feel it, *now*, within me. Nothing else matters as much. I don't need to be *right*, I don't need to be *heard* – I need peace. Now!" And then, withdrawing your awareness from the outer world, go inside to that place where peace abides and allow yourself to *feel it*! It is always there waiting for you to 'quicken' it into greater and greater waves of peaceful power. It's that simple. But you must go to that inner place again and again, leaving all other desires to quiet down and dissolve. You *can* do it if you want to badly enough."

From From the Heart of a Gentle Brother, High Mesa Press, Taos, NM 87571.

Meditation and Prayer

Have you ever wondered about the relationship between prayer and meditation?

Meditation done with faith in the Absolute is a form of prayer. From the beginning of Christianity there has been a tradition of contemplative prayer. There is historical evidence that Jesus and the fathers of the Christian faith were very familiar with and used the ancient meditation disciplines.

The Bible presents meditation as a way to become aware of the presence of God's spirit within us. It says that meditation can be practiced by any sincere person. To do this you stop looking for the ultimate reality outside yourself and get in touch with the presence of God within. Then, you may experience the reality of eternal truth and the Absolute.

Meditation is in accord with all religious schools of the world. The goal is the same for all – to bring yourself to the experience of God.

The death-resurrection experience, the dying and rebirth which is at the heart of Christianity, is part of the meditation process. The mind becomes quiet, there is a dying of the false self – the ego, the superficial self. Then the true Self, which is God within, can be reached.

When the authors were growing up, during the 1920's and 1930's, in different parts of the country, each of us had the same problem with prayer. Each of us thought, "There must be some formula for prayer that I don't know." There was a constant fear that we weren't doing it right. There was always a sense of pressure that we were supposed to measure up to some standard, and we didn't have any idea what the standard was. The harder we tried to pray, the less we were able to do it. And, of course, none of our prayers ever seemed to be answered. As a result, each of us stopped trying to reach God through prayer.

When the authors first came in touch with meditation, it was not as a form of prayer. Meditation was introduced as a way to transcend daily life, quiet the ego, and get in touch with the power of the subconscious mind. Using meditation as a form of prayer came later. It was as if the idea of reaching God through meditation sneaked up on us. It just happened. By the time we realized we were reaching God through meditation, our old fears about not being able to pray in the right way were gone. Somehow we had gone beyond the form of our original praying and had reached God directly through meditation.

Since we don't know exactly what happens in the meditation experience, it is difficult to describe it. We quiet the body and mind, and we reach God. Our usual consciousness is suspended and the presence of the Spirit can be felt.

We are also finding, more and more, that the experience of God stays with us beyond the time spent in meditation. When we come out of meditation, the connection with our Higher Self, a sense of being one with the Source, lingers on in other parts of our lives.

In summary, meditation and prayer both take us into that peaceful, joyful, direct experience of the Higher Self. The way to reach this calm, centered place within doesn't matter. God doesn't care if you come by sitting quietly, by focusing on your breath, by saying a mantra, or by any other meditation or prayer practice. Whatever your practice, the most important thing is taking the time to reach God within.

184

Turning on Your Power
Through Networking

Now that you have played with the "Peace Diet" for a while and have meditated and visualized world peace, you may want to combine your energy with others through networking.

A network has been defined as "a pattern of human interaction characterized by a process of information exchange usually leading to other human interactions and/or material, service, information, monetary, or spiritual exchange." (Richard Haight)

Networking for peace is a phrase used in the widest sense to describe individuals who are making connections with one another to spread information about peace. Networking for peace involves talking to others about peace, sharing inner and outer accomplishments, and exchanging information with one another about what is going on in peace-related fields. Joining together in small groups can lead to significant human interactions and powerful spiritual exchanges. It is a way to become more actively involved in making peace a reality on our planet.

We know peace will come through the intention and commitment of many individuals to make this a peaceful world.

Krishnamurti summed it up when he said, in part,

"To rely on others is utterly futile; others cannot bring us peace. No leader is going to give us peace, no government, no army, no country. What will bring peace is inward transformation which will lead to outward action."

This is true. Peace comes first from within each one of us and spreads outward to embrace others.

Making contact with others in the networking process creates a group reaction which releases your combined energies. These energies form a synergistic bond for spiritual awakening that results in positive change for everyone. Today this spiritual awakening is spreading through the efforts of everyone involved in the peace movement.

We don't know how soon world peace will occur, or how many of us are needed to make it happen. We do know that it is already in process and, ultimately, the change *will* take place.

Becoming part of a networking group to work and be with others of similar vision is a powerful experience. It feels like coming home. You aren't alone anymore as you realize your dream of peace is a shared reality.

A very valuable by-product of networking is trust. People start trusting each other when their inner selves make contact. They realize on some deep level that they can count on one another for support. As we join with others to meditate and visualize peace, a powerful transformation occurs. And as time goes on, all the shared experiences of combining energies and spirit develops into unconditional love for one another.

We noticed this during our first organized networking experience, a weekly group meeting to meditate and do processes for inner peace. In our group, each person's higher self seemed to speak, and the voices blended to become one Voice for Peace. The combining of individual energies created one bright beam of light, radiating peace into the world. Perhaps Jesus had in mind the synergy of blending separate parts to create a greater whole when He said, "Whenever two or more are gathered in my name, I am there."

Millions of people on our planet have a deep yearning for peace, and through our individual and combined efforts, world peace *is* becoming a reality. Robert Muller, former Assistant Secretary-General of the United Nations, summarized the networking process this way:

"Decide to network
Use every letter you write
Every conversation you have
Every meeting you attend

To express your fundamental beliefs and dreams.
Affirm to others the vision of the world you want.
Network through thought.
Network through action.
Network through love.
Network through the spirit.
You are the center of a network.
You are the center of the world.
You are a free, immensely powerful source
of life and goodness.
Affirm it.
Spread it.
Radiate it.
Think day and night about it
And you will see a miracle happen:
the greatness of your own life.
In a world of big powers, media, and monopolies,
But of four and a half billion individuals,
Networking is the new freedom
the new democracy
a new form of happiness."

From Planet of Hope, by Robert Muller
Amity House, Inc., Warwick, New York, 1985

Promoting Peace with Resonating Core Groups

This book was written to open the door for greater inner peace and unconditional love. Many people are on this same path. More and more, these people are communicating with each other and meditating together. We have been in various groups over the years which have been invaluable in sourcing our own inner peace.

One of our groups is called a Resonating Core Group. A core group meets weekly for several hours over a period of twelve weeks. Group members take turns leading the sessions in a leaderless format. Judy Cranmer wrote the following about the core group experience:

> "Resonating Core! For me, it means a sharing of group energy as we connect with our Source which is Love. Our meeting begins with a silent meditation during which we each contact our Higher Self and the power of each of us is amplified into a synergistic force far greater than the individual. We resonate with this energy.
>
> "This is followed by a guided meditation during which I reach a state of separation from

ego. I float free and unencumbered. As I meditate, I write in my journal feelings from my essence. There is time and space for both verbal and non-verbal sharing as we draw closer to each other. I become us.

"My heart opens to embrace each member of the group, and we close with our arms around one another in a circle of Love, expressing our thoughts and feelings. This resonation carries me through the week on a high note, and I take each member of the group with me. Our journey together has begun."

If the core group process appeals to you, consider starting a core group yourself. Begin by contacting two or three friends or business associates and selecting a mutually convenient time and place to meet each week for the coming three months. You need not be a leader to start a group.

A booklet, <u>Resonating: An Introduction to the Core Group Process</u> is available to assist you in starting a group. A manual for the twelve weeks is also available, entitled <u>Connecting at the Heart: Manual for Building a Global Community</u>. These publications are available from Global Family, 305 Cowper Street, Palo Alto, CA 94301, (415) 323-4999.

Bibliography

The Aquarian Conspiracy, by Marilyn Ferguson. 1980, J.P. Tarcher, Inc., 1910 Sunset Blvd., Los Angeles, CA 90069.

The Awakening of Intelligence, by J. Krishnamurti. 1973, Krishnamurti Foundation Trust Ltd., London, England.

A Book of Games, A Course in Spiritual Play, by Hugh Prather. 1981, Doubleday & Company, Inc., Garden City, NY.

Celebrating God's Presence, A Guide to Christian Meditation, by William E. Hulme. 1988, Augsburg Publishing House, Minneapolis, MN.

Choices and Connections '88 – '89. Human Potential Resources, Inc., P.O. Box 1057, Boulder, CO 80306. Annual.

Connecting at the Heart: Manual for Building a Global Community. 1988, Global Family, 305 Cowper Street, Palo Alto, CA 94301. (415)323-4999.

A Course in Miracles. 1975, Foundation for Inner Peace, P.O. Box 635, Tiburon, CA 94920.

Daily We Touch Him, Practical Religious Experiences, by M. Basil Pennington, O.C.S.O. 1979, Doubleday & Company, Inc., Garden City, NY.

The Evolutionary Journey, A Personal Guide to a Positive Future, by Barbara Marx Hubbard. 1982, Evolutionary Press, 2418 Clement Street, San Francisco, CA 94121.

The Flame of Attention, by J. Krishnamurti. 1984, Krishnamurti Foundation Trust Ltd., London, England.

From the Heart of a Gentle Brother, by Bartholomew. 1987, High Mesa Press, P.O. Box 2267, Taos, NM 87571.

Good-Bye to Guilt, Releasing Fear Through Forgiveness, by Gerald G. Jampolsky, M.D. 1985, Bantam Books, Inc., 666 Fifth Avenue, New York, NY 10103.

Happy Birth Day Planet Earth, The Instant of Co-Operation, by Barbara Marx Hubbard. 1986, Ocean Tree Books, P.O. Box 1295, Santa Fe, NM 87504.

I Come as a Brother, A Remembrance of Illusions, by Bartholomew. 1986, High Mesa Press, P.O. Box 2267, Taos, NM 87571.

Illusions, The Adventures of a Reluctant Messiah, by Richard Bach. 1977, Delacorte Press/Eleanor Friede.

I May Not Be Totally Perfect, But Parts of Me Are Excellent and Other Brilliant Thoughts, by Ashley Brilliant. 1981, Woodbridge Press Publishing Company, P.O. Box 6189, Santa Barbara, CA 93111.

Jonathan Livingston Seagull, by Richard Bach. 1973, Avon Books, 105 Madison Avenue, New York, NY 10016.

Life Ahead, by J. Krishnamurti. 1963, The Theosophical Publishing House, Wheaton, IL.

Living in the Light, by Shakti Gawain. 1986, Whatever Publishing, Inc., 58 Paul Drive, San Rafael, CA 94903.

Love is Letting Go of Fear, by Gerald G. Jampolsky, M.D. 1979, Celestial Arts, 231 Adrian Road, Millbrae, CA 94030.

Loving Each Other, The Challenge of Human Relationships, by Leo Buscaglia. 1984, SLACK Incorporated, 6900 Grove Road, Thorofare, NJ 08086.

Manual for Co-Creators of the Quantum Leap, Version Two, by Barbara Marx Hubbard. New Visions, P.O. Box 5102, 3051 S.E. 35th Street, Gainesville, FL 32602.

Meditation in Christianity, by Swami Rama/Rev. Lawrence Bouldin/Justin O'Brian, D.Th./Father William Teska Arpita, Ph.D./Sister Francis Borgia Rothluebber/ Pandit Usharbudh Arya, D.Litt. 1983, The Himalayan International Institute of Yoga Science and Philosophy of the U.S.A., RD 1, Box 88, Honesdale, PA 18431.

New Genesis, Shaping a Global Christianity, by Robert Muller. 1984, Doubleday & Company, Inc., Garden City, NY.

New Teachings for an Awakening Humanity, by Virginia Essene. 1986, Spiritual Education Endeavors Publishing Company, 1556 Halford Avenue, #288, Santa Clara, CA 95051.

The Other Side of Silence, A Guide to Christian Meditation, by Morton T. Kelsey. 1976, Paulist Press, 1865 Broadway, New York, NY 10023.

Peace A Dream Unfolding, edited by Penney Kome and Patrick Crean. 1986, Somerville House Books Ltd., 24 Dinnick Crescent, Toronto, Canada M4N1L5.

The Peace Catalog, edited by Duane Sweeney. 1984, Press for Peace, Inc., 5621 Seaview Ave. N.W., Seattle, WA 98107.

Peace is Within Our Reach, by Sri Swami Satchidananda. 1985, Integral Yoga Publications, Route 1, Box 172, Buckingham, VA 23921.

Peace Trek Family Coloring Book, by Joel and Diane Schatz. 1986, Ark Communications Institute, 250 Lafayette Circle, Suite 202, Lafayette, CA 94549.

The Planetary Commission, by John Randolph Price. 1984, The Quartus Foundation for Spiritual Research, Inc., P.O. Box 26683, Austin, TX 78755.

A Planet of Hope, by Robert Muller. 1985, Amity House, Inc., 106 Newport Bridge Road, Warwick, NY 10990.

Practical Spirituality, by John Randolph Price. 1985, The Quartus Foundation for Spiritual Research, Inc., P.O. Box 27230, Austin, TX 78755-1230.

The Quiet Answer, by Hugh Prather. 1982, Doubleday & Company, Inc., Garden City, NY.

Steps To Prayer Power, by Jo Kimmel. 1972, Abingdon Press, Nashville, TN.

The Superbeings, by John Randolph Price. 1981, The Quartus Foundation for Spiritual Research, Inc., P.O. Box 26683, Austin, TX 78755.

There Is a Place Where You Are Not Alone, by Hugh Prather. 1980, Doubleday & Company, Inc., Garden City, NY.

There's No Such Place as Far Away, by Richard Bach. 1979, Delacorte Press/Eleanor Friede, 1 Dag Hammerskjold Plaza, New York, NY 10017.

With Wings as Eagles, by John Randolph Price. 1987, The Quartus Foundation for Spiritual Research, Inc., P.O. Box 27230, Austin, TX 78755-1230.

Order Form

- All orders to be prepaid. Please add $2.00 shipping for first book and $1.00 for each additional book.

- California residents add 6-1/2% sales tax.

- 10% discount on orders for 5 or more books.

- Detach this completed form and mail with your check or money order to:

    Right Brain Unlimited Publications
    P.O. Box 160484
    Cupertino, CA 95016-0484

- Make checks payable to RBUP.

Please Print

Name: _____

Address: _____

City: _____ State: _____ Zip: _____

Phone (optional): (_____) _____

The Thirty Day Peace Diet: send _____ x $9.95 = $ _____

Plus 6-1/2% sales tax (California residents only) = $ _____

Plus shipping for ONE book (U.S. only) = $ ____2.00____

Plus $1.00 for each additional book sent

    to same address: = $ _____

TOTAL ENCLOSED: = $ _____